COMMUNITY WORKERS

A Doctor's Job

PATRICIA DAWSON

Cavendish Square

New York

Published in 2015 by Cavendish Square Publishing, LLC
243 5th Avenue, Suite 136, New York, NY 10016

Library of Congress Cataloging-in-Publication Data

Dawson, Patricia.
A doctor's job / Patricia Dawson.
pages cm. — (Community workers)
includes index.
ISBN 978-1-62712-990-9 (hardcover) ISBN 978-1-62712-991-6 (paperback) ISBN 978-1-62712-992-3 (ebook)
1. Physicians—Juvenile literature. 2. Medicine—Juvenile literature. 3. Physicians—Juvenile literature. I. Title.
R690.D385 2015
610.92—dc23
2013050625

Editorial Director: Dean Miller
Editor: Amy Hayes
Copy Editor: Wendy Reynolds
Art Director: Jeffrey Talbot
Designer: Douglas Brooks
Photo Researcher: J8 Media
Production Manager: Jennifer Ryder-Talbot
Production Editor: David McNamara

Printed in the United States of America

Contents

Doctors take care of people who are healthy.

Doctors take care of people who are sick.

Doctors make sure you feel your best.

I listen to your **chest.**

I can hear that your heart is healthy.

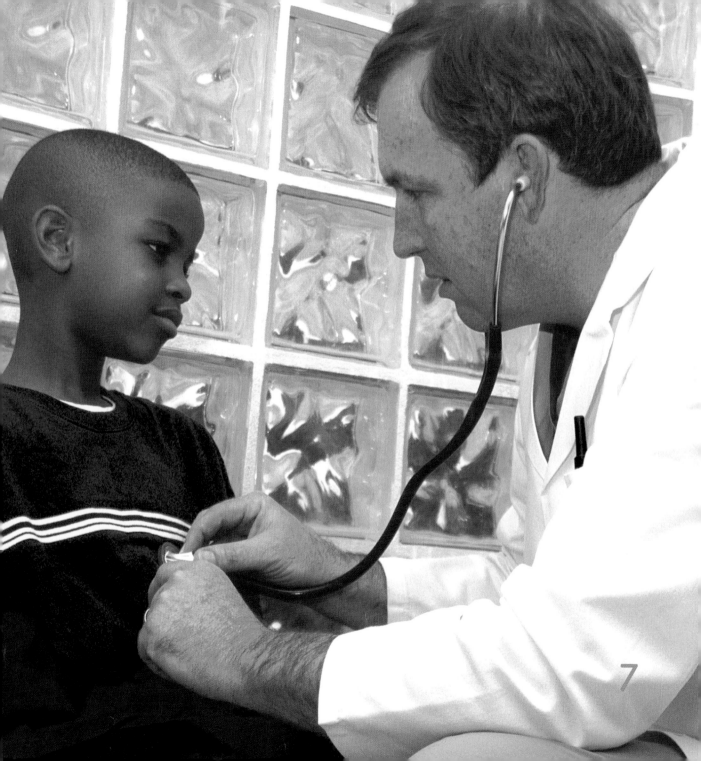

Open wide and say, "Ah."

I check your throat and **tonsils**.

I make sure that they
look healthy.

I look inside your ear with
a light.

I check that your ear
looks **normal**.

I make sure that you
are growing.

I find out how tall you are.

I check how much you weigh.

13

Are you not feeling well?

I need to **examine** you to see what is wrong.

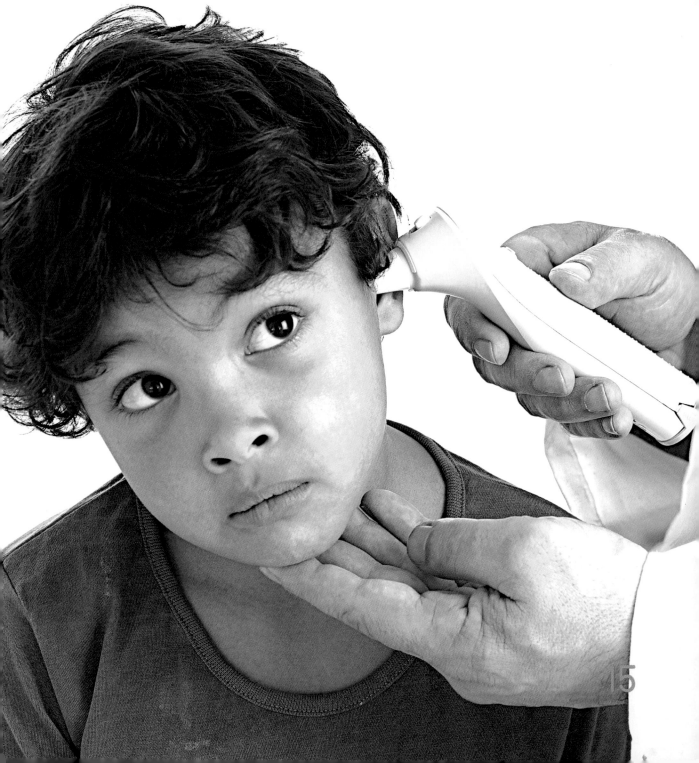

Does your head feel hot?

I take your **temperature.**

You have a **fever.**

This **medicine** will make your fever go away.

17

Sometimes you need a **shot.**

This shot will keep you healthy.

19

Everything is fine.

You are healthy.

I will see you for another
checkup next year.

Words to Know

checkup (**chek**-up) a visit where a doctor checks to see if you are healthy

chest (**chest**) the front of your body

examine (ig-**zah**-men) to look at closely

fever (**fee**-ver) when your body feels warm because you are sick

medicine (**meh**-duh-sin) something given to help you feel better when you are sick

normal (**nor**-mul) healthy

shot (**shot**) medicine that is given with a needle

temperature (**tem**-per-achur) tells you how hot or cold you are

tonsils (**ton**-sulz) two small parts on the sides of your throat

Find Out More

Books

Ask Nurse Pfaff, She'll Help You!
by Alice K. Flanagan, Children's Press

Doctors Help People
by Amy Moses, The Children's World

My Doctor, My Friend
by P. K. Hallinan, Hambleton-Hill Publishing

Website

Daniel Tiger's Neighborhood
pbskids.org/daniel/games/doctor

Index